Conceptions of LOVE

A Poem of Undying Love

BY DR. FLORENCE DAVIS GREEN

(CEO, Ordained Minister, Mentor, & Poet)

WestBow Press books may be ordered through booksellers or by contacting:

WestBow Press
A Division of Thomas Nelson & Zondervan
1663 Liberty Drive
Bloomington, IN 47403
www.westbowpress.com
1 (866) 928-1240

Scripture taken from the King James Version of the Bible.

ISBN: 978-1-5127-1926-0 (sc)
ISBN: 978-1-5127-1927-7 (e)

Library of Congress Control Number: 2015918561

Print information available on the last page.

WestBow Press rev. date: 11/20/2015

WESTBOW
P R E S S®
A DIVISION OF THOMAS NELSON
& ZONDERVAN

To Jesus Christ be the Glory!

"For God so loved the world, that he gave his only begotten Son, that whosoever believeth in him shall not perish, but have everlasting life" (Biblehub.com-KJV, 2015, John 3:16)

Contents

Rev. Dr. Florence Davis Green's Favorite KJV Bible Verses

"Let the words of my mouth, and the meditation of my heart, be acceptable in thy sight, O LORD, my strength, and my redeemer" (KJV Bible-Biblehub.com, 2015, Psalm: 19:14)

&

"Precious in the sight of the lord is the death of his saints" (KJV Bible – Biblehub.com, 2015, Psalm: 116:15)

&

"..greater is he that's in you, than he that is in the world"(KJV Bible- Biblehub.com, 2015, 1 John 1:4)

&

"If we confess our sins, he faithful and just to forgive us our sins and to cleanse us from all unrighteousness" (KJV Bible – Biblehub.com, 2015, 1 John 1:9)

&

Blessed is the man that walketh not in the counsel of the ungodly, nor standeth in the way of sinners, nor sitteth in the seat of the scornful. But his delight is in the law of the LORD; and does he meditate day and night. And he shall be like a tree planted by the rivers of waters, that bringeth forth fruit in his season; his leaf shall not wither and whatsoever he doeth shall prosper (KJV Bible – biblehub.com, 2015, Psalm 1:1-3).

&

"The thief cometh not, but for to steal, and to kill, and to destroy: I am come that they might have life, and that they might have it more abundantly" (Biblehub.com-KJV, 2015, John 10:10).

&

"Jesus saith unto him, I am the way, the truth, and the life: no man cometh unto the Father, but by me" (Biblehub.com-KJV, 2015, John 14:6).

Reverend Doctor Florence Davis Green's History

Reverend Doctor Florence Davis Green was the Chief Executive Officer and founder of Peacemakers in Charleston, SC. Peacemakers is a nonprofit organization which caters to helping needy people. Some of the services that the firm offers are hot plates of food, prayer, mentoring and others. For over 45 years, the CEO fed people in the Charleston, SC area, visited nursing homes, assisted hungry people and offered various types of help. Reverend Doctor Florence Davis was born in Charleston, SC between the year 1934 and 1936 on March 27. She was the wife of Otis Green, and the daughter of Abraham Davis and Beatrice Saures Davis. She grew up in a home of discipline with her siblings as Ernestine Davis Grant, George Davis, Johnny Davis, Thomas Davis, Paul Davis, Eugene Davis, and Abraham Davis, Jr. She was awarded three doctoral degrees as PhD in Ministry, DBA in Leadership, and EdD in Christian Studies - though departed. She was the ordained minister who preached the King James Version Bible for over 40 years at various churches like her last one at New Christian Missionary Baptist Church on Magnolia Road in Charleston, SC. Also, she married numerous couples, counseled families, communion people, taught Sunday school, and prayed for numerous entities. Reverend Doctor Florence Davis Green was well known to those who she assisted in the Charleston, SC area. She was a poet and wrote from her heart. The poem in this document reflected the way that she felt about love. She passed away from this earth on March 16, 2015 between the hours of 5pm to 7pm in her home where she worked. She leaves the world with a very intense poem which ignites the emotions of one's soul.

Conceptions of Love

Love is of God. God is Love. He firsts loves!

That is why all humans must first -- love someone or something.

Love is eternal!

It is everlasting!

Love is stronger than death!

Death is limited, but love is not!

When we love someone – mother – wife – child – or friend and he or she dies –

Does the love we have for them die? Or, does it deepen at the thought of them being gone away for always?

And- Sorrow has filled our hearts. And- the longing of being with them once more.

Love is consistent of many special things such as a deep – penetrating – over-joyous feeling and a passionate – burning desire of wanting of or for someone – (a person).

It is invisible, unseen, and can't be heard. Unheard of, but you can feel it.

Love is as the wind.

Can't be seen but felt.

Knows not how

or where it comes from

or when it will come upon you suddenly.

Strangely, unexpected and strongly - as though some unknown goodness has dealt with your soul.

Love is not made. It is created.

Made from something.

Created is from nothing.

It just happens.

The time appointed at creation is of the creator – God Almighty!

Love makes one feel inferior at times. Not being the right person for the one he or she loves.

That person feels much below his or her mate at times.

At other times, a feeling of superiority is deeply felt such as
   I am just as good or better than he or she.
   And - the person that's in love
   will feel in his or her
   highly emotional state of feelings.
The other person involved is lucky to be loved by him or her –
   - and that person is more important
   - than his or her mate.
Some people go through life and find love at an old age.
   Some find it while they are young
   and realize it
   and build upon it.

It is as a small seed! It must be fed and treated daily to further its growth.

Much affection and tender loving care and attention much be had. For when it is grown, it is the greatest seed of all.

No, there is nothing greater and nothing was ever made or created – even was meant to be greater than love.

Sometimes, one may say – I am not in love anymore – the feelings are gone.

If once in love – always!

The feelings have died down

-that you may be able to bear it.

If that overpowering feeling remains always – we will die from it.

So it is taken for a while so that we may
be able to bear it.

As one may kill his or her feelings
----- if love is neglected
It will soon die – itself
if not nourished!
We can live -- ever so long without food
or water.
So – also
love can live a while without being
fed ---
and it vanishes as it came.

God love is beyond human understanding!
His love remains even after ours die. Human
love alone is not strong enough. We need
God's love to further our love.

That ---
may
become
that lasting and undying love.
The poor falls in love
the rich,
and all that can breathe.

God is Love! So he has blessed all of his creations to partake of his love. Creation like humans feel love.

It respects no one.

Love so is –God!

God is no respecter to a person or things.

Love is smell! The beauty and sweetness of it. Love is taste! Tasting the sweet joy of passions and ecstasy of honey-flavored joy!

Love can see all of what it loves and blind to all else.

Our senses are taste, the same as love, smell as love, see and feel as love. It is the control of our very existence. It is the control of our very being.

So when love is going well, we are happy because

that love

that controls all

- is well.

When things are not right – something goes wrong -- for some reason or another.

We shrink and we're unhappy and want to die. Here's why – because our control is out of order.

Love is sharing – unselfish and understanding

– trying with all one's heart and soul to understand the reason, thought, or motive of a loved one

- and realizing that we must remember to look below the surface.

For every action there is a reaction. Put yourself in his or her place and size up the matter or situation.

Love is longsuffering as soon as things don't please one

-he or she sometimes give-up.

Suffer – bear whatever must be bear. For as long as it must be.

You feel like giving up – keep fighting – stick with it – never give-up.

Love is endurance. Stick with what must be suffered. Never give-up!

Love is tolerance. Put up with it. Take it - until there is no more to take.

For when you feel it's the end at the breaking point – God takes over.

You feel it's the end – well it's the beginning of endurance!

God never puts no more on anyone than they can bear.

The stronger one feels for another – that much more must he go through or suffer.

Are you worthy of that true love? You will be tried, time and time again and proven.

Love is faith – working together – with all of its attributes and wonders of life.
Love cannot be seen.
You may see the one you love,
but that love
that is working
so powerfully within
– cannot be seen.
So is faith.

Faith is the proof
– assurance of things hoped for.
A conviction of things not seen.
Why should a man hope for that which is seen, but hope for that which is not seen?
As long as one lives – there is hope that anything may yet take place in life for him or her.
We have faith, hope, and love.
The greatest of these are LOVE!
Doubt not.

Printed in the United States
by Baker & Taylor Publisher Services